Explore the magical world of unicorns in this enchanting coloring book! With pages filled with beautiful illustrations of unicorns in stunning landscapes, each image awaits to come to life with your favorite colors. Let your imagination soar as you paint these majestic creatures and create your own realm of fantasy!

This Book Belongs to:

Test Color Page

DV Publications©

DV Publications©

DV Publications©

DV Publications©

DV Publications©

DV Publications©

DV Publications©

DV Publications©

DV Publications©

DV Publications©

DV Publications©

DV Publications©

DV Publications©

DV Publications©

DV Publications©

DV Publications©

www.ingramcontent.com/pod-product-compliance
Lightning Source LLC
Chambersburg PA
CBHW080547260726
48663CB00008B/461